Hues of my mind

Nirupama Choudhury

© **Nirupama Choudhury 2022**

All rights reserved

All rights reserved by author. No part of this publication may be reproduced, stored in a retrieval system or transmitted in any form or by any means, electronic, mechanical, photocopying, recording or otherwise, without the prior permission of the author.

Although every precaution has been taken to verify the accuracy of the information contained herein, the author and publisher assume no responsibility for any errors or omissions. No liability is assumed for damages that may result from the use of information contained within.

First Published in June 2022

ISBN: 978-93-5611-556-9

BLUEROSE PUBLISHERS

www.BlueRoseONE.com
info@bluerosepublishers.com
+91 8882 898 898

Cover Design:
Muskan Sachdeva

Typographic Design:
Sachvesh

Distributed by: BlueRose, Amazon, Flipkart

Table of Contents

1. Good Morning! 2
2. Facets Of Summer
   - I 3
   - II 4

Emotions 5

3. Sometimes, I Wish 6
4. A Mistake 7
5. A Dried Leaf 8
6. Ugly 9
7. A Child In Me 10
8. A Race With Time 11
9. Equality 12
10. Breathing Hope 14
11. The Devil In Me 15
12. The Music In Me 16
13. The Metamorphosis 17
14. An Old Dark Soul 18
15. A Call For a Succor 19
16. I Wish 20
17. Dark 21
18. My Neighbour & I 22
19. The Mismatch 24
20. Tea & Dark Evenings, ... 26

21. A Sleeping Seed 27
22. The Fences 29
23. Dwarfism 30
24. A Gloomy Painting 31
25. The Journey 32
26. Quiet Nights 33
27. Far Away 34
28. A Wave 35
29. Frozen 36
30. They Said 37
31. Flowers and I 38
32. Rejuvenation 39
33. Old Frames 40
34. Bad Weather 41
35. Facets of me 42
36. A Vagabond 43
37. Truth and Lies 44
38. A Desert 45
39. Mysterious Sac 46
40. Buried Alive 47
41. Forgiveness 48
42. Stuck 49
43. Easy Sayings 50
44. A Scorpion 51
45. The Banana Leaves 52
46. Flight 53
47. My life and I 54

48.	I can do it	55
49.	The First Purchase From Time	56
50.	Writing Poetry	57
51.	Empathy	58
52.	Blaming	59
53.	Fading Relationships	60
54.	A Push	61
55.	My Monsters	62
56.	Home	63
57.	Solitude & Isolation	64
58.	It's Okay To Be Delicate	65
59.	Escape	66
60.	Dreams	67
61.	Fiery Birds	68
62.	Music	69
63.	Waiting	70
64.	A Place of my Dreams	71

Raining Metaphors **73**

65.	Life; A Bridge	74
66.	A King	75
67.	A Golden Cage	77

Feminism **79**

68.	They Said	80
69.	Period	82

Patriarchy **83**

70.	A Decent Wife	84
71.	Our Kingdom	85

72.	Wings of fragility	88

Freebird 89

73.	A Winged Bird	90
74.	Winged	91
75.	She	92
76.	Shades of Gray	93
77.	The Cliff	94
78.	Caged-I	95
79.	Caged-II	96
80.	The Fall	97
81.	Rise	98
82.	Wounds	99
83.	Walking Grave	100

Covid Times 101

84.	The Quarantine Times	102
85.	Stay	103

Love 104

86.	A Need For Fostering	105
87.	A Need For Fostering	106
88.	Everything, but Love	107
89.	Drafting Consolation	108
90.	You And I	109
91.	What Is Love?	110
92.	If I Could…	111
93.	Gravity	112
94.	Burnt	113
95.	Tinted Glass windows	114

96.	That Someone	115
97.	Monsters	116
98.	Love Dome	117
99.	How old is your love?	118
100.	With the wind	119
101.	When you come	120
102.	Memories	121
103.	Will you be mine?	122
104.	My Muse	123
105.	Frozen	124
106.	You	125
107.	One Liners	126
108.	Truth Platter	127
109.	Ode To My Best Of Pals	128
110.	Don't Come too Close	129
111.	Flattery	130
112.	She is Wild Waters	131
113.	A Goal	132
114.	Walkers Of Life	133
115.	Paralysed	134
116.	Weight	135
117.	I Wish To Be Found,	136
118.	A Miser,	137

Poems Of The Season

1. Good Morning!

The breaking dawn looks serene,
As serene and silent like a secret,
That was sleeping under the quietude of the night,
With the music of the rustling trees,
And the lullabies sung by the winds.
These winds traveled miles:
Through houses and streets,
Woods and countries,
Carrying stories of various species,
Only to balm the serene secret to sleep,
Till the fog gracefully wanes,
And a new dawn arises!

2. Facets Of Summer

I

The summer matures, slowly,
With the waving golden paddy plants,
As farmers return home reaping crops from their fields,
Then the noon prepares to leave,
After feasting on them,
Leaving them soiled, sweaty & weary,
The ravens caw,
From the roofs of the buildings,
Lotuses doze,
As the ponds tire after submitting itself to the fiery sun,
Mirroring its mood, since dawn,
Finally, it mercies upon us with solitude,
Leaving us drugged with lethargy,
To rest for a while,
Till cows moo,
That return to their shelters,
Ringing the bells on their leashes,
Then, my thoughts are rowed,
Towards the seasonal mangoes;
A bunch of joy that hang on luscious green trees,
That invites me for a gala feast,
& the green ones smile at my sour teeth,
That are picked to be pickled,
In the hustle of the evening!

II

The Summer

The summer ages,

With our constant desires to be released,

From the captive of its heat,

To be free like the chilled winds of the morning,

But, as the blazing noon up rises,

It burns everything with it;

The grass, the trees, the roads, the houses, the people & their hearts,

It behaves fanatic,

As if there was a spell of a dark magic,

To whirl hot winds, to put the wild on fire,

To split the Earth,

While the weary farmers wait to be Merced upon,

With their tanned bodies & hope!

Cities rustle & hustle,

With a nostalgia of their childhood memories,

Of ripe mangoes, plums, berries & lots of love,

With a longingness to visit the countryside,

Being locked up, under a roof, hot,

They peep through the blue tinted glasses of their windows,

To get some hint of clouds,

But they are left with an itch, that couldn't be scratched,

And we ponder,

That summer holidays are there, indeed,

Of which they are least enjoyed.

Emotions

3. Sometimes, I Wish

Sometimes,
All I wish is to become a child again,
Curled up in someone's arms,
By folding my knees to my chest,
And be caressed gently,
As smooth as the barbs of a feather,
To be protected from the harsh world,
Like a seashell that shields its pearl,
To be nourished with warmth,
Like an embryo,
That grows in a mother's womb.
And cry my heart out,
To a father who would listen to my vocally inarticulate voice,
Who would stand like a pillar,
To defend me from the outcries of the world,
To be touched by the rays of the first sunlight,
That strengthens my nerves and bones,
And the adrenaline in me rushes,
To wake up with the armors of courage!

4. A Mistake

I lived in a surreal world,
Holding the cumbersome weight of fear in my heart,
To be manipulated,
To be alienated,
To be abandoned,
To not be accepted with love/care,
For being different from others,
Until one day a bell rang in my head,
It was the voice of my subconscious self,
That was stuttering hard to say,
That I was actually shattered to nothingness.
The fear that I had always scared to face,
Had spread its reign far and wide,
And I have a few moments to lament,
For allowing the pains disguised in peace,
To build an empire in my heart.
Unable to stand its weight,
I broke to different personalities,
The colors of life changed dramatically,
When looked through different views,
But it was the same for me,
Except Black and Gray,
As those were the only hues I could see.

5. A Dried Leaf

I am like a dried leaf,
That falls as the winter's grief,
While the house of destitute hails me in,
Emptiness crushes me from within.

6. Ugly

I was ugly,

Because I mirrored honesty,

I was weird,

Because I was not a songbird,

But a voice of protest,

I showed vulnerability to resist wrongdoings,

I was an image of truth,

Like a clean delicate mirror,

That got cracked,

When stones of hatred were thrown upon.

The cracks embroidered the fierce anger, abuses, allegations and questions on my existence,

But never broke my authenticity though,

They shone in its own pride,

Each one with its own glamor,

Representing the angst of mankind,

And this broken mirror shone like never before,

I looked at myself in despair,

To find that I turned beautiful!

7. A Child In Me

There lives a child in me,
Whose feet is always set to flee,
Far away from the noise of the city,
Escaping from the paradoxical laws of order,
To a vast field of poppies,
Where she could run around wild and free,
Racing against the birds that fly over her,
Chasing squirrels that peep out of some tree holes,
And glide around their trunks in glee,
Then she would climb up to the branch of a tree,
Hang from it upside down,
And listen to the echoes of her own laughter,
Basking under the setting sun.
The passing clouds, the waving poppy flowers,
The balmy wind, the playful animals,
The kind trees, and the blissful solitude,
Would welcome innocence in its true spirits.
The artless truth and honesty,
That act wild like a carefree child,
Would be sheltered.
Panting, she would stretch to fall on soft couched grass,
And then, breathing the air of joy,
She would be aided to fall asleep.
To wake up to the age-old painful reality,
Far alone, again in the city of hypocrisy.

8. A Race With Time

Every day, I take part in a race with time,
With no intention to win,
But to move in the same pace,
And to be with it in the same space.
Then, I speak to my muse,
Time keeps moving like its very nature,
Like a tortoise that crawls towards its goal,
Pulling through all weathers.
It leaves me behind in silence,
While I am consumed by my thoughts,
To arrive with a novel piece of work.

9. Equality

I thought that we were born equal,
And lived in that thought,
Until I stepped out of my house to see,
That some people were strong and some were weak,
Or was that only in my mind?
Some were hiding their bodies in disgust,
While others were looking at them with lust,
I thought that we were born equal,
Or was that just a thought?
One day someone asked me,
If I would be his date,
Only if I told my figure,
I couldn't figure to figure what this "figure" meant,
Until he told me that it was the physique that I carried with me,
Along with my heart, mind and soul,
The courtesy of manners defended me,
To ask the same question to him
And I thought that we were born equal,
Or was that just a thought?
I lived with a little hope from the mankind,
Then,
I was told that I am born beautiful,
And the size of the body and complexion didn't matter,
Then, why was I teased if I was short,
And I wore heels till my legs hurt,
Neither were my eyes big,
Nor my lips pink,

In the places that I ever crossed or lived?
I thought that the beauty laid in the eyes,
And we were born equal,
Or was that just a thought?
I wonder whom would we please,
Or would seek pleasure from,
If the world was blind,
I think, if we could give this thought a thought,
Probably, my thoughts wouldn't remain only as thoughts!

10. Breathing Hope

I am trying to fit into a mold,
Where, my spirits just don't set,
 Willingness fear to touch the base,
And happiness condenses.
It has become my routine,
To go against the wind,
I am scared, if my courage sinks,
For it has wrecked my enthusiasm little by little with time,
And I just breathe hope, to survive.

11. The Devil In Me

There lives a devil inside,
In the cells of my mind,
It talks loud when I prepare to start my day,
And is awfully quiet when I challenge its survival ways,
It grows bigger as I ignore it to the core,
And let my lethargic senses linger,
Till it freezes my thoughts like it was winter.
I envy its quirkiness,
That breeds inferiorities within,
For it becomes bigger than me,
And mocks at my inabilities.
Then, it enters that peaceful cell,
That lay in oblivion amidst all,
Like the serpent that entered God's paradise,
To sin the sleeping sinless.
All my nerved faculties wake up to that noise,
To put my wisdom on guard.
So that it could work in peace,
And the devil inside is stilled.

12. The Music In Me

I am a song of melancholy,

Its lyrics composed by my life,

Feelings bring the rhythm,

Emotions play the beats,

As my thoughts set the tone.

When the tone, the beats, the rhythm, and the lyrics come in harmony,

I become a song of melancholy.

A song,

That tells stories of the unsung hearts,

Connects with the music of the souls,

And I keep singing every day, honing my art,

Changing its beats and tones.

I am not as rejoiced as a melody,

Yet, the music upbeats in me,

To travel beyond countries and cities,

And settle in the hearts, and enshrine in the minds of many.

Mind you, I am a song of melancholy!

13. The Metamorphosis

Sometimes I wonder:
What happened to the I in myself?
A child whose charms were her cheerfulness,
Had metamorphosed to distress?
A star that enlightened herself and others,
Has fallen by her flaws?
Growing up was knowledge,
Yet, seldom did she ask for her better scores,
She cherished other pursuits,
That involved her inner self more,
A bright spark but in academics,
Dolls play seemed stereotype,
But, not the stories of werewolves,
She was amiable in her own ways,
Not an anomaly,
Her innocence befriended several curiosities,
Some let her bloom with knowledge,
While others left her damaged,
However, to survive a victim of prejudice,
Didn't seem upright, but amiss,
The breakdowns never made any sound,
And with time, she blended into the background.

14. An Old Dark Soul

I feel, I am a darker shade of gloominess,
Bathed in the amalgamating smoke and quietness,
Of the burning dead,
As the kohl from the smoke settle on my skin,
I take pride in sprouting the wings of fragility,
Like the Achilles's heels,
For, I am an old dark soul,
That uplifts itself,
When it is sheltered by darkness.
While I am ecstatic to laud the sufferings,
I am also grounded by the gravity of anguish,
To burn and perish,
To rise again from the ashes of my sanguine spirits.

15. A Call For a Succor

I could have helped you,
But, the life in me is so wildly restless,
To sneak out of this hollow being,
To leave the aching body and mind,
That my conscience seems to have lost,
Raging a war against my mind!
I wish, I could have helped you,
But, my unsteady feelings abruptly rise and fall,
When I make efforts to drive my zeal along,
For, I thought to find beauty in me,
But before I could venture inside,
The demons within would eat me up like it suffers from gluttony!
I wish I could have helped you,
But my own charms of life are wearing off.
Would it become volatile?
Or, would it empty me like a parasite?
Or the monstrous chains would tighten,
Ultimately, to liberate me, to free me from myself?
I wish I could help you...

16. I Wish

How I wish,
I diminish,
In a fraction of a second,
And blossom for life
The next moment!
How I wonder,
Stoicism clutches me,
And the hope for better days stands still!
The quietness around, seeking answers, speaks to me,
And I respond with silence loudly.!

17. Dark

There is a dire need to be invisible,
Till the unseen me ceases to eternity,
After I had survived the suffocation,
Breathing the air of despair in my mind's prison,
Anxiety, peeps in and hides out with time,
Playing gingerly with my mind,
Like a dear friend of mine,
Ironically, that's such a rare thing to find?
Like the furious winds of the world,
I feel so whirled,
With my thoughts that are constantly at war,
With itself and against the conscience,
That all I wish is this force of life,
To be stopped!

18. My Neighbour & I

The moon and the stars,
All my neighbor,
From my terrace, close to a harbor,
We exchange glances,
While talking in silence.
When darkness lays,
Tides rise,
With the surge of my feelings,
My aims sigh,
If I could settle with ease,
Convinces the cool breeze,
For the city looks congested,
With ambitions & failures,
On coffee tables and some office premises,
Some homeless on roads,
Some in the balconies of their houses,
Some on rooftops, like me,
"But, no woes can live,
To the calming notes of the waves,
That dashes on the eternal shore,
Where you can lay back secure,
Away from the urban colonies
At least, invisible to the eyes?",
Persuaded, the essence of the landscape,
Yet, could I be as selfless as my neighbor?

My greedy self seals a deal,
With the giving nature,
That it would come back seeking its company,
When its soul is at unrest.

19. The Mismatch

We have:
A quest for love,
With hands full of conditions!
The days' light that harms nature, a plight,
Is the same that awakens & nurtures life,
Our life foggy,
Yet, we can write books of advice!
A wish for a guide,
For the mysterious life,
Yet, adventures sway their ways,
& Mysteries are fun, they say!
Emotions strong,
Yet, a humane company is none,
Deep being small talks!
Felt lonely,
Yet, solitude offered to be the best bonhomie!
Power, which isn't a need,
Guarantees security!
Many responsibilities,
Feel like burdens!
Declared ourselves free,
Feeling caged from within.
Done countless good deeds,
But, feeling appreciated was the only shortcoming!
Sunrises beautiful,
Yet, we wait for night falls,
To embrace darkness,

Yet, it leaves you to grieve alone as time crawls,
When the heart is heavy,
With recurrent thoughts.

20. Tea & Dark Evenings,

I have learnt to gulp my sorrows in dark evenings,
With freshly brewed tea & my feelings,
When silence is the only conversation I have,
Caused by the noises in my mind.

21. A Sleeping Seed

Autism was growing its root deep,
Silently, in the core of my mind,
Laying the speech faculty to sleep,
That was disturbed by its exposure to the reality, bathed in prejudice,
And it slept like a sleeping seed.
Then, I was born,
Unique,
With the inability to voice my opinion out,
I locked myself up in the dark,
That gave me a thin skin,
And with overly exposed nerves,
I shut myself from the calamities of reality,
From choosing a path to walk on, to live,
That lay ahead, among many.
After eons, as I decided to step out,
The doors of bravery creaked,
The long sleeping self-respect screeched,
To wake up to a new reality,
Confidence stood as feeble as my shaky feet,
And with no emotional balance,
I held wrong hands to stand upright,
Till I realized how miserably I had fallen.
The very thoughts of these failures,
Felt as traumatizing as a brain vegetated in a body,
To analyze how submissive I had been all my life,
And I learnt, that fairies live such low lives as their tales,

That waiting for a miracle will go in vain,
To uproot the uniqueness that I had been living with,
Pretending death,
To turn me into a hero someday.
But those failures,
Taught me that I can be the charioteer of my own life.

22. The Fences

With the fences of uncertainties around,
I walk in the dark, every day,
With a hope to be touched by light,
And I long to feel high,
Like a playful child,
But my ever wandering eyes encounters only darkness,
As my chancy steps trod towards life.
Sometimes, I bump into closed doors,
While at other times, those fences mend to make ways,
Weary, I cringe, cry and yell in my mind,
In solitude that shelters my woes.
I fear if this darkness spreads to the self within,
It would infect the hope,
That would turn me blind.
These fences are amongst those immortals,
That see the world ahead of me,
And eclipses my sight in a competitive psyche.

23. Dwarfism

While I still gather pieces of myself,
To stand upright, grounded,
Concurrently, being moved by the wheels of reality,
My dreams, soaring somewhere high in the sky,
Call me from above to be addressed,
Weary, from the labor since dawn till the dark,
To build a strong and better me,
I retire, every day, looking up with regret,
For, they have been shining like the brightest stars,
Since the day I saw them,
And they followed me consistently,
No matter my slippery feet,
Or, if I ever climbed heights,
Like a promise kept,
But, I couldn't stand tall enough,
To catch them,
To travel along!
While they pity at my dwarfness,
Every day, I bury myself within me in disgrace!

24. A Gloomy Painting

My life looks like a gloomy painting,
Stilled and dejected, yet craves attention,
The hardships in it stand like stubborn rocks,
That block ways for light to enter,
I move forward with all my will and sanguinity,
With the rotating and revolutioning earth,
To reach success,
That stands with pride on the land of happiness,
But, I find myself stuck at the same place from where I had started,
After numerous attempts,
I see myself in a state,
Where I couldn't distinguish,
If my fate designed this reality,
Or I stand in the middle of a puzzle in my nightmare,
When, I am being pulled back by the winds,
And the crabs beneath, grab my steady feet,
I wait for this mysterious scene to unfurl its charms,
And set me free,
To march towards the goal I aimed for,
And the roads ahead to look clear,
So that I could walk with great dignity and my valor,
For I would have crossed the forests of uncertainties then,
And paved ways for my future,
With the light of my experiences and perseverance.

25. The Journey

In the journey of life,
Walking on steep roads feels like a fall,
The hills need patience and are painstaking to climb,
While the plains end in no time!
I am neither a follower in a herd,
Nor a Shepard that leads with pride,
From the back, doing his duty,
But a wanderer,
That is inspired to become both, with a purpose,
To walk on a line that leads to destiny,
A path that has the treasure that keeps me happy,
No matter the roads; slopes, hills, plains, slippery or shabby,
And at the end of it, it has a pot full of a drink,
Made with a priceless thing called content,
To quench the thirst of it,
To reward the weariness, effort and the zeal for a firm feet,
When being hit by rocks in the dark.
I know, I have miles to walk,
With only a wish for a light,
To cast my shadow,
A learning to reflect upon,
The key to the treasure,
And a company along,
While I walk alone.

26. Quiet Nights

Sometimes, I plead the quiet nights,
That haunt fearful souls,
To take some of my quietude too,
That is burdened with the weight of my grief,
To merge with it and build itself scarier,
And then, embrace me tight so that I can weep louder,
That would camouflage the echoes of the dead,
Then, there would come a time,
When neither the spirits dare to be awake,
Nor a living creature sound,
I would pray for it to wait,
Till the gush of my pain is lowered,
With my pillows wet,
Till I could hear myself,
And stir the quietude.

27. Far Away

I want to travel far,
Far from the human essence;
The sinned, by nature,
And go so far,
That I become aloof to knowledge, wisdom and judgment,
And reach a place,
Where a bleeding heart is balmed,
And as the love chemical shower,
Sorrows drain away,
Where I am drugged by a caressing hug,
& I fly weightless, like a soft feather,
Such an ecstatic space,
I wish to be crafted by the almighty again,
Just like the Eden garden,
Where I meet the incorrupt, innocent, solitude, and peace;
The priceless gifts in a bundle,
That we wait lifelong to receive!

28. A Wave

I move like a calm wave of a sea,
Carrying a huge inconspicuous storm within,
Emotions gush to flood my heart out,
But the walls of despair suppresses the desire,
Then, I fall back to rest like a sea weed,
For ages, assured of the prevailing darkness,
Yet, unsure of my bulging heart,
That tows me from sleep with its weight,
And I look up seeking answers,
To know, if I could ever rise to the light.
If I could create ripples around,
And change the fate of the sea,
Or I would merge with the rhythms of the reality,
Or hit the ground,
To bounce back to the point where I could start again,
With a newborn force and winds of wisdom around.

29. Frozen

So many winters,
All in a year,
I grew colder with the hail storms of life,
And died of emotional vacuum,
Longing for warmth from a hearty being,
From the fathoms of the place,
Where my life was buried,
And all I saw were masked entities,
Who sang love songs,
But, to distance myself from the lost.

30. They Said

They said to move on,

But did they build a reservoir in their hearts too,

To hold my pains when they shower?

Did they lay empathetic lands,

To soak my sorrows,

As they flooded, breaking their capacity barriers?

They said to not become weak,

But, did they soil their hands in crafting me as myself?

They said to adjust and sway,

Per the winds of reality,

But, did they teach me to be a human?

When I was turning stoic,

Persevering the blows of life?

Or were they been humane to my innocence,

When I didn't have the answers to my vulnerabilities,

They said a lot of things,

Following the superstitious social norms,

But, it would have been a lot better if they had only said, "it's okay",

And accepted me with my anomalies.

31. Flowers and I

Rebellion could be the new rhythm,
& I like flowers,
So what?
If the world outside is burning with a rage,
I often dream of a quiet place,
Trying to find myself in the foggy newness,
& Let the fair winds touch my skin,
That had been longing to be free,
From the shackles of prejudiced minds!
You know, I have always liked the flowers,
That bloom carefree,
Just like the child in every being,
It's only on some occasions, my mind is on an articulating spree.

32. Rejuvenation

When everything falls apart,
I look for darkness,
To consume me,
Where I could disappear into the thin air,
& fly with the wind,
That blows towards the forest that is green,
Where I could breathe life again,
And start building a new reality,
With more strength & firm will.

33. Old Frames

The mistakes of my past echo,
And knock at my memory door,
To mourn the loss of the precious.
I close my eyes with a sigh,
And embrace myself in the graves of my heart,
I stare into the abyss that films every details of the former me,
And as the frames pass,
The sea of grief within, surges to swell,
To wash the skin off, painted in shame.

34. Bad Weather

I am struck amidst a bad weather,
Where I lay heavy on the worldly ground,
I long to embrace cheerfulness,
But, all that I could afford is,
Only to pull through the adversaries,
And with every breath, I decide to leave,
Yet again, I pat myself to fight,
To grow wise with time to live.

35. Facets of me

Sometimes I feel that I am a bomb,

Ready to explode, destroying everything around, along with me,

While at other times I feel as if I'm as calm as the sleeping waters in a deep sea,

With my toes at the extremes,

I let darkness to swallow me,

Yet, I couldn't turn a blind eye to the gray fields,

That builds itself like a stubborn scar,

Against my emotional wall,

In my private space that homes solitude,

Then, there comes a moment when I'm so powerful so as to defeat the strongest foes,

And then, I also turn so fragile so as to shatter to uncountable pieces, before the clock ticks a tock.

36. A Vagabond

Being a Vagabond,
I had stepped into the houses where I knew that I didn't belong,
Cold, longing to be wrapped with warmth,
& to be caressed with gentleness,
But, the air inside was filled with indifference,
I mocked at the silence,
And in response I heard my own feet tread towards nothing,
There were little panic strokes,
But I didn't lose hope,
I thought the residents would be courteous enough,
To at least ask about my well-being,
But I learnt that I was mistaken,
When I choked by suffocation,
Breathing same air for long,
I rushed to the entrance door to catch my breath,
And that very moment I felt,
That the world outside had more oxygen,
Than the space I ran into for life,
It was cold, calm, tranquil and freezing everything to asleep,
Yet it strengthened my bones to walk gracefully,
I resumed walking, turning stoic with time, but in love,
With the freezing self and the ice outside,
Appreciating the art of nature,
Relishing the songs the cold winds sang with all heart,
Till I turned to a piece of art.

37. Truth and Lies

Truth is not an art,
A lie is,
And we have beautiful artists around,
Who mesmerize us with their art,
Alas! We have the heart of a playful child!

38. A Desert

A desert can soak abundantly,
Maybe, so much so that it can quench its thirst and then,
Store underneath,
To give it to the one who comes looking for it,
But, only if the rains could trust.

39. Mysterious Sac

I'm a sac full of mysterious things
A grave within to bury my sins,
A smile for the visitors,
A frown inside, struggling to make its way.
Sometimes, mocking at my restrained capabilities,
Life whistles out of me,
Holding the pressures of expectations within,
Either placed by me or by somebody,
Yet, I manage to breathe,
With an aging hope,
In dire need of a wand,
To set me free.
Such tiny a creature,
And I aspire to be crowned in a sky,
Imprinted with the pictures of my failures,
On my skin,
Counting the days for a sunrise.
Voices battle within,
Till the persevering one makes it till the end,
Alas! Could the powerful helplessness be as majestic?
As a good king be?

40. Buried Alive

I am buried while alive,
I struggle to breathe,
Amidst the darkness,
And the Earth seems to have stopped rotating,
Hence, the place I reside have only nights,
And my breathlessness is far from the vision of the light,
My voice couldn't cross the rocky layers of reality,
And no air pass through the pores,
I stay immobile,
Fathomed to believe,
That I am blinded to foresee,
If I would ever decay to germinate,
Or it would take me eons to die.
I strive for a glimpse of light,
Of all the time lapsed,
With a prayer to be forgiven,
But I don't know,
If my voice would ever rise through the soil to above.

41. Forgiveness

Forgiveness smells like,
A withered rose,
As light as a cologne,
That disappears into the thin air,
With your indifference to the past,
As you breathe life,
Of a refreshing present.

42. Stuck

I push hard everyday,
Yet the mountain of hardships doesn't move an inch.
I feel suffocated,
Crunched by the space where I don't belong,
I peep through the windows,
To breathe freedom,
At least for a moment,
My wings set to flap naturally,
As you open your arms to hug your loved one,
But chained by helplessness, they couldn't rise,
And then, I wish to die,
But the anticipation of regretting hits again.
I am turning stoic slowly,
Like the moisture in cold air turn to ice,
With the passing time.

43. Easy Sayings

It is easy to say;
To stay calm,
To stay strong,
To be positive,
It would rather be better to lend arms & empathy at times,
When uncertainties blow the castle off, you built in your dreams,
Every time, you climbed heights to give it life.

44. A Scorpion

If only a scorpion could walk out of her nature,

That is always restless, swift & agile,

Like a buzzing gray flickering screen on a TV screen with no signal,

Her walk would have grace,

Her endeavor would become constant,

Things would have been distinct to her eye,

Albeit, a clear aim would still seem to be at a farther space,

She would have been more determined,

Like the tortoise in the race,

Her stings would have been colder and stronger,

On those who attempted to stamp on her unique personality,

Or,

She could convert her poison to her fuel,

To push her forward like good winds,

She would be kinder to her peers,

& Indifferent to crabs.

She wouldn't be lost in the woods,

But decisive of her walks in her life.

45. The Banana Leaves

I wonder if my life is like the banana leaf,
That swings with the winds,
Right next to my house,
Luscious green, a treat to my eyes,
That wait to be plucked,
But torn by the winds,
In the course of time,
Who enjoy the rain equally,
As the tall, plain, straight, untouched leaves do.
The broken ones dance to the winds together,
Embracing indifference shown by the humans,
Like their very nature,
While the virgin ones remain unmoved & stand tall with grace,
Only to be cut,
To become a platter,
And serve a human stomach;
A basic need for life.
Then it perishes,
As the hunger is satiated.

46. Flight

In life, you fly
Light & cheerful,
With a ballooning ego,
As you soar above slicing the clouds of fear,
One after the other,
Winning over hardships,
Flying over dead circumstances,
Over caging fences,
Till you are weighted with your flaws again,
You halt at a rock,
Life brings you a mirror,
To show you the dirt that you carried along,
And you take a step down to clean yourself,
That takes a while,
Till you are grounded,
You shred all your ego, subconsciously,
Like a snake,
That leaves its dead skin behind,
And you are ready for a new flight,
With your innocent & fearless wings.

47. My life and I

I am someone,

Life seems to be another being,

That passionately wants to play my enemy,

Who constantly keeps a watch on my rise,

& like a crab, pulls me down every time I climb,

I put all my efforts to free myself from the clutch of the crab's feet,

Alas! I am left with pitying myself,

Being a part of such stubbornly continuous events,

I realized that I should learn to grow thick & spiky skin,

To elude myself from those who don't belong from my kin,

That wait for my fall,

As time crawls.

That I should keep my efforts up to push myself,

No matter my heavy feet,

My consistent willingness to achieve shouldn't shrink,

With my strength, being clenched,

I shouldn't fade away with darkness.

I should rather leave my enemy behind in the race.

48. I can do it

I think I didn't give my best yet,
I know I'm not just a common stone,
I'm yet to shine,
I'm yet to change the history,
I know that I can reach beyond my thoughts could command,
I'm an achiever & a dreamer,
My dreams would grow younger,
I will walk beyond my expectations,
I'm yet to show my best.
And I know it,
Otherwise, I won't be thinking about it,
I am yet to shine,
I'm better than your perception about me,
I'm yet to show it.
The day I turn over all the stones,
You will find a gem,
I will wear a crown of pride,
I may then turn deaf to the noises around,
As the voice within would sing & relish the songs of my victory.

49. The First Purchase From Time

The first thing that I bought for myself was :
Ignition,
With barely a thousand rupees in hand,
& Countless dreams in my eyes,
I walked with a heart of fire,
Towards the road that lead me to be rich,
I earned a living,
& A little more,
Taking my folks along,
I walked miles,
Till I learnt that I am yet to buy more.
& Keep buying till I am content with what I had bought.

50. Writing Poetry

Writing poetry is a way to rain the clouds,
That once hovered over you,
Giving birth to the songs that you were pregnant with,
Holding your deep emotions for long enough,
Embracing your real self with content,
In front of the mirror,
That the words just built for you with honor.

51. Empathy

I wish happiness fell from above,
In small packets,
On days when you are gloomy,
You discreetly want to be loved,
And wish your beloved ones were as intelligent as smart technologies,
To sense your sorrows,
Before anybody else could do,
Without you telling them about it,
Then, they would wrap you in a hug,
Filling the empty jugs you hold,
That poured love, once,
From the tank of your heart,
Now, heavy by an emotional vacuum,
& you transfer some of your gravity in return,
To be pulled up from your lows.

52. Blaming

Blaming others for your mistake is like,
Fermenting the guilt chemical,
Till it becomes a regret,
And you gulp the final substance,
Being tipsy with the poison inside,
You hallucinate holding a dagger,
With misery dripping from it,
That stain the face of the murderer,
Who killed your morale,
And shows you the pictures,
Of your actions in the past,
Framed one after the other,
Just in the right order,
Mirroring the memory of a strangely beautiful mind.

53. Fading Relationships

Ironically, when tied to an emotional bond with variety of rules,
After a day's stay in it,
When I close my eyes
I fall from the edge of worldliness,
As light as a feather,
Renouncing from the gravity of wisdom and rightfulness,
With no desire to be pulled by a parachute,
But to touch the ground bottom with ease,
Serene and content,
But I'm being woken up by a new sun,
And I have to rise, weighting intelligence,
To fit in a so called bond,
Joined by hands, each different from another in its shape and style,
Striving for unity,
Surviving itches, cramped, with time till the day retires.
When I just start to relish my failures.

54. A Push

Time is racing,

I'm stuck,

In the whole reality of today,

Empathizing with my aspirations,

Adjusting with the shortcomings of today,

Stemming hope for perfection,

With a turbulence inside,

I stink of my clogged dreams,

Sometimes pulled by the strings of responsibilities,

Sometimes I bow down in front of my weaknesses.

I don't know how to proceed,

Scared to be stuck again,

Yet, at the end of the day,

I tell myself: One hard push is a lot better than rotting in a foreign space.

55. My Monsters

Where do I hide my monsters,
When everyone wants to see perfection,
I am scared to scare the ones I care for,
With my imperfections, flaws, darkness and anomalies,
Albeit, I am a free bird,
And not a clone,
I suffocate being masked,
Hence, most often I live alone.

56. Home

Home is a place where we fly to, to find happiness,
Ironically, that's where pain creeps into our nerves.
Then, we move far,
Stretching the physical distance,
To find solace in a chaotic race,
Somewhere in a so called well-mannered society,
That lives in masked arbitrariness every day,
With a smile to project,
Like a time bound effort,
Resecting themselves from being available,
To acknowledge your tender feelings,
Unlike home that bail your tensed emotions.
But, you neither want to rush home,
Which lives in its true essence, vulnerable and raw,
Nor you want to cut ties,
As, deep within you know,
That the thought of breaking the nothingness of the unreasoned stretched distance,
Still hurts like a menace.

57. Solitude & Isolation

Life is such an irony,

At times, when you are away from your dear ones,

You are so rich with loneliness that you want to spend time with family,

And when you are with family,

You want to go away,

As your emotions are bankrupted,

Consumed by everyone else's heated thoughts.

58. It's Okay To Be Delicate

It's okay to be delicate,

You break instantly after every fall,

Yet, you hold the strength to stand again in one piece,

Assembling all your broken pieces,

Unlike the strong ones that hold the pain for long,

And break like never before,

That fall silent, or with an alarming noise,

That none expects of,

Sometimes unable to comprehend the situation,

Zoned to denial,

Sometimes living different emotions at extremes, like a versatile actor,

Locked in the cage of his own mind,

Changing hues of the self, subconsciously,

Till someone accuses him of a disorder in disguise,

Of a Pleasant man, but unwise.

59. Escape

The I in me wants to screams loud,
And deafen the surrounding crowd around,
Desperately seeking solitude,
In a quest to speak to my muse.
How cleverly my mind plays with me,
When I am alone,
I long for a company,
To be embraced by an amiable society,
Now that I live amidst them,
I want to run away.

60. Dreams

Dreams come like reels,
With some photographs missed in between,
We try to connect the scenes,
Only after a new sun shows light on our brain's memories.

61. Fiery Birds

Some fires ignite souls,
Some burn the dead,
I have burnt myself,
When my house was on fire with the elderly's rage,
With the fuels of ego, misunderstanding and unnecessary verbal shoots,
Tears often rolled off my cheeks,
To soothe the agonizing questions on my existence,
I was growing stoic to be resistant to this prevailing heat,
With the spreading fire, they burnt themselves too,
Wearing masks of smile, desperately,
To rush away from each other,
To breathe some fresh air,
In search of worldly things in the name of freedom,
Dumbed to feel that they were caged by their hollow mind,
That was heated by flames of hatred & indifference,
When I tried to douse the fire,
They replied that they have the right to be free,
Every day, portraying some or the other lame reasons to escape.
I spoke to my muse: one who is free, always soars high,
And she doesn't seek excuse,
To fly away,
As her wings are unstoppable,
No matter where her nests lay,
Either she lives alone or with her flock
She flies with dignity,
Freedom is her nature,
And not a gate to cross to find it.

62. Music

The music around was pleasant as usual,
I was missing among the notes,
I tried to play along,
But an extra note wasn't the need of the hour,
& when I found that I don't fit into the rhythm,
I set my own tune,
And played the flute.

63. Waiting

Waiting is like an abyss,
That you are bent to stare at to find nothing,
You stay there immobile like a standing mummy,
And breathe the present,
That clutch your hands & legs from moving,
Patience fill the air around,
& you live on it to survive
Till time rings the bell
And release you from a static psychic bound.

64. A Place of my Dreams

I wish to be found,
Amidst the time,
Where gravity only would mean to fall down while playing,
With cackles of laughter in the air,
Followed by band aids worn on hurt knees,
Cheery, sportive, artless,
Naive to the miseries of reality,
Or the worldly Pleasures.
Without being pulled in by the web of feigned treasures.

Raining Metaphors

65. Life: A Bridge

Life is that bridge,

That connects innocence to wisdom,

And all in between, lays the journey of learning,

Where we either run, stumble, wait or walk,

As the road ahead unfurls the moments of joy, pain, patience, or sorrow.

Hollow space underneath,

And vast emptiness above,

Like a zero around,

That expects you to build things in it,

Beautiful;

Like memories, experiences or history,

No matter the things, you must cross the bridge,

Either living it as a grief or a bliss.

66. A King

There lived a King,
Chivalrous, sportive, adorable, and majestic,
Who always returned home with cheers of his victory,
From harsh battles,
Sometimes pleased, sometimes hurt,
Either ways, he wore the crown of pride,
That let his pains subside.
The enemies he fought with,
Were pregnant with cruelty, foolishness & catastrophe.
They died without purging,
And gave birth to inhumane, destructive, unpredictable things,
That grew stronger than their parents,
& waged wars against the king,
Who kept fighting for his kingdom,
Until age wore his mind too,
With the aging hope, seeking peace,
Like a last wish,
Till the day, he lost the way to the battlefield,
The dwarf, pernicious creatures hunted for their prey,
To find him paralyzed, laying weak in a jungle,
They shot him on his head,
& broke his crown,
By then, the king had already lost faith in his own strength,
He laid there, quiet & lost,
Like a vegetable,
Rotting each day,
Unable to measure if his past deeds were virtuous enough,

That would bring his kin looking for him,

And inject him with love,

To wake him up from an anesthetic stupor.

Is it a plight to say that,

A celebrated king once, lay there lost?

Or it's time to wonder if God would mercy him with bravery, again,

So that he rises to a greater height than a living man's reach, with pride?

67. A Golden Cage

One day I was sitting quiet on my writing table,
Leaning to the window,
Staring at the empty sky for inspiration,
To write something new,
Holding my pen and a blank sheet,
& the ink from the inkpot evaporated to space,
On a windy summer afternoon,
Until you perched on my table,
Carrying clouds of hope,
Only to shower on me,
And as you shredded the weight off,
You looked at me innocently,
As if you were sent by angels,
To meet only me,
In the world,
With a divine purpose,
To dress me with heaven's love,
I knew instantly that you were precious,
And with the fleeting time,
You took the shape of my poem,
I tried to keep you in the safest chamber of my heart,
Without realizing that you breathed freedom,
You hammered all the walls,
Trashed the doors,
& broke the entire house with all your strength,
While I was busy creating chandeliers for you in my poetry,
I was dumbed to give a heed to your rebellious efforts,

& you flew away quietly,

I longed for the guest in my distorted house,

As my tensed nerves busted,

Unable to find the trace of yours,

My sanity went haywire like the crazily hanging roots out of a giant tree,

Till I realized that I was in love,

And in the effort of keeping you safe,

I caged your soul.

Feminism

68. They Said

They said that I was the Emblem of strength and perseverance,
But did they recognise me when I was being consistently the same,
Unsaid,
But they did question me,
If there was no progression in my performance,
They said that household chores should be my priority,
And I should follow the norms of the society,
But did they come to defend me,
If the society changed its own guidelines?
Ironically, they also said
That I was born special,
Then, I wondered;
Why celebrate it just one day.
Then I recalled some names like Shakti Mohan, Priyanka Chopra, Shreya Goshal, Chanda Kochar, Kalpana Chawla, Kamla Das, ...
And all the beautiful women out there,
Who chase their dreams,
Breaking the glass ceilings built by these people,
And then,
I told them,
Like you, I have my burning desires too,
May be, neither to flaunt femininity,
Nor to be a hero in a group,
But to plant the seeds of equality in the minds of those,
Who decides how the world should be.

Today, I take pride in what I do,
Shattering the walls that the society built,
Along with other queens here,
Who fix each other's crowns.

69. Period

My legs sore,
As if the nerves in them got tangled,
Like several thin wires,
That were pulled fiercely from a cable,
My moods fumbled to react,
With its swift swings, it couldn't choose one to act,
The spine & the back sighed in agony,
Like it towed a heavy thing,
I sensed a turmoil in my uterus,
As if there was a push & pull of a flesh,
& in the wake of the cramps,
A liquid bomb exploded,
And its particles flowed towards an edge,
But, before they could fall off,
I pleaded them to stop for a while,
Till I get a tampon,
& then my head started to ache,
Rushing for this mission,
It's then the particles united as the grief of the uterus,
Said in a chorus:
"I am coming",
I pleaded it again to hold it till I pee,
But this time it adamantly whooped: "stop all the drama,
& Here I come"- Period!

Patriarchy

70. A Decent Wife

She unveiled her pretty face,
That flushed once,
Admiring her spouse's presence,
Her eyes glistened with happiness,
Head down,
Shying away from the novel society,
That only wondered at her wandering mind!
In the inhumane sands of time,
Her dreams turned to nightmares,
Every night, she shuddered from her maiden stupor,
Till fear nerved her to be a pleasing wife,
The peaceful tears that laid silent in her body,
Flooded up to wash all her aspirations away,
And all her desires sank in the sea of sacrifice.
The struck red and gray marks
On her gentle skin,
Led to a cancerous heart,
Her soul was burnt in a boisterous hell,
Until her thoughts and emotions were turned to ashes,
And then,
She woke up every day as a death in life!

71. Our Kingdom

Many times I had not loved my parents,
Like I was an illegitimate,
Sometimes, bound by the limits of my age,
Succumbed to all my rage,
I cried, to not to be heard,
But to communicate my vulnerability to myself,
Every night my pillow read my mind,
As I laid my chaotic emotions at rest, sighing.
It sympathised at my fragility,
When I woke up to the nightmares of a dysfunctional family,
Patriarchy was sitting high,
Like a Satan on its Pandemonium,
Proud of its mistaken supremacy!
And I was aspiring to be a princess,
In my King's palace,
However, a woman who took care of the king's people,
Was never given a crown,
And I believed that I lived in a kingdom!
A similar residence that I also saw in cinemas,
And around, in the society I grew,
Where Queens never spoke their mind,
If they did, their thoughts were slayed,
By sharp insecure male egos,
With both their voices and hands high,
Hence, it became an unsaid rule,
To be pleasant to men,
Irrespective of how hard they criminate you,

To submit yourself to manhood in every kind,
Be it serving them food or listening to their woes,
"A woman survives only when her man does",
Thus, said my mother.
I listened to her in disdain,
To understand, how gracefully she sacrificed her life,
In return for nothing,
As if she was born to submit herself to a man,
And teach her daughter to abide by the same rules,
That she was taught once,
A mandatory course that I should learn,
That my school didn't teach,
While my other siblings of the male gender,
Are free to say & do as they want.
Today, my parents are old,
& I don't hate them,
But succumbed to abide by those rules at home,
I cry, again, to not to be heard,
But pitying those who are tormented by the tantrums of men,
Today, I am strong but incapable,
Wired to suppress opinions,
I passively talk about equal rights,
And given deaf ears,
Even when I scream for it actively,
Denial is what I get in response,
My thoughts seem incomprehensible to my fellow beings,
I am seen as non-religious,
As I oppose the tradition,
Patriarchy is looked at with respect,
Like a religion, sacred,
And this culture is passed on by my ancestors,

To the sapiens of today's generation,

Who couldn't reason why one gender was considered sacred everywhere,

And the other one only at temples.

72. Wings of fragility

Blooming under the Realms of patriarchy,
I thrive with a longing for chivalrousness,
Laborious with the maiden name,
Weary, being decked up for a society,
That expects you to pose in a certain way,
My thoughts soar in the sky,
To fly to my second home someday.

Freebird

73. A Winged Bird

I was born free,
I knew that the sky was my nest,
But I didn't have wings,
So, I played with my peers,
And learnt to walk on the ground,
Then flapped my tiny feathers,
And fluttered around.
Until one day,
I slept for long,

And woke up to see,
Clouds full of fear above,
I screamed for help,
But rains wiped my pains away.
I struggled hard to push the clouds away,
Thenceforth, the sun shone,
And my ignorant eyes opened to see,
That I was only dreaming and
Caged by my own mind!

74. Winged

I am empowered to have the wings,
Built by my persevering mind,
That lived consistent hazards, thrown by life,
To escape to an unknown space,
Sometimes to the unvisited rooms of my thoughts,
While at other times into some tangible ones,
Where I could meet some cheerful faces,
Or, at least those who feigned happiness,
To trade my innocence with peace,
Swiftly, to not acknowledge,
The harsh blows of adversaries,
That battered my limbs weak,
With hard & ugly realities,
Every time, I struggled to stand,
Wearing age and loneliness with time.
So, I soar high,
Invisible, from the grounds of reality,
Sometimes, I perch,
On the edges of extremes,
Only to fly off the cliff.

75. She

She was art,
Free as waters of a stream,
You collected her in a glass,
And she took the shape,
You let her flow,
She painted stories,
Her charms attracted visitors,
But to pass by,
You caged her,
And her soul flew with artistic wings.

76. Shades of Gray

It feels quite heavy these days,
As if growing old was a curse,
Happiness flew away with time,
& I ponder over the cloudy reality,
Longing for a good laughter,
To be lost & fly ecstatic into nothingness,
But, along with my body, knowledge grew in me too.
Days of chaotic silence,
Question me about my wings,
I drown & dive with the tide,
Hoping to be touched by good winds.

77. The Cliff

I had jumped off the cliff many times, with people,
With trust, all decked up in innocence,
I had broken myself so many times,
That the pieces that I hold together,
Now, speak, that they lack the ability to break anymore,
When I had climbed up here again,
But to tell them that, this time I will not fall,
I will fly with the wings of my memory shades.

78. Caged-I

Caged in their thoughts,

My wings tore,

Every time I tried to fly,

Was hit by their mockery on my weaknesses,

That burnt something inside me,

Like a chemotherapy,

Then, like a pulley,

I'm being pulled by strings of imposed jobs; framed under responsibilities,

Till I weigh heavy with pain,

I turned back ugly,

With a clenched feet,

Till darkness put a halt to everyone's busyness,

I laid down there in peace with gravity,

Till my dreams flew away from the windows.

79. Caged-II

Being constantly pulled back,
By the tender emotions of my dear ones,
I lost the strength to fly,
Blinded by their conflicting ego,
They said: you are free,
I smiled artistically
And took a flight into my imagination,
To release my tightened nerves,
From my tense mood in isolation.

80. The Fall

I ran towards the cliff,
Escaping from the monsters of dark,
Panting, and tearing up the rock,
Till it came close to my face,
I looked down to see that I was standing on the edge,
And a deep ditch below to embrace my fall,
I closed my eyes & jumped into nothing,
Only then, I realized that I can fly with my courageous wings.

81. Rise

I want to rise above,
And float in the darkness,
Sit close to the brightest star,
Enjoy the view of my world from far,
And look at the things down,
That weighted my flight;
The envy, the competition, the egos,
To rise above and beyond that light
Where gravity doesn't exist,
I look down,
To give a treat to my eyes.

82. Wounds

Why does it always happen that when I long to be loved,
I touch only the broken,
And the broken break me too,
With their sharp indifference,
And they cut straight my heart with their treachery,
Initially with quotes of love,
Later, by belittling my love,
I don't understand,
If they couldn't move on, being extremely fragile,
Or I had been blind all this while,
Who couldn't see that I had gone too far,
Trying to pour love,
From an empty jar.

83. Walking Grave

People buried their sins in me as if I were a walking grave,
Like a priest in a church,
Who offers absolution?
I questioned my identity,
For I was looking for a young soul,
Like a blooming rose,
To accompany me in the journey called life,
To be drenched in the worldly pleasures of life,
Before I get dried to soak in others' woes.

Covid Times

84. The Quarantine Times

I am trying to find focus,
In the midst of exhaustion,
With a hope for resurrection of mankind,
In the times of quarantine,
When the mother Earth is healing,
From the rampage it was enduring,
From decades till date.
And I find it difficult,
To put in just a limited effort,
In keeping hope, staying home,
And remember the pained in my prayers,
For the better times to come.

85. Stay

There is a curfew of hope,
With my sanguinity being locked up,
By a deadly virus,
That flew from a foreign land,
To my land of prosperity and growth,
Spreading its tentacles far,
Gradually, infecting my fellowmen,
Building its dome,
Terrorising my innocent home!
A battle with it and a battle within,
So much for a human to fight,
Being home,
Weapons of patience & tolerance are honed,
And they are stroked on fear & anxiety as they approached!
Poor intellectuals of the Earth,
Who didn't ask for more,
But happiness and peace,
With their routine chores and a little more,
Who never imagined this massacre,
Stay,
No matter what,
Feeling lamed or constantly taming your hearts,
In the battlefield,
And thrive with an inconspicuous mental stigma,
United by care and cleanliness,
But at a distance,
Combating its hostility,
Unaware of the longevity of the crisis!
Stay.

Love

86. A Need For Fostering

Please don't leave my hands, when I am fragile,
Don't set me free, when I am wild!
Pull me close when it is cold,
Shower me with love when my demons spit fire,
One day, I will be your nightingale,
In the disguise of a sparrow,
And I will commingle in you,
Having found the gem,
I will sing the song of the hidden treasure,
And fly carefree,
Sprinkling the priceless love from above.

87. A Need For Fostering

Please don't leave my hands, when I am fragile,
Don't set me free, when I am wild!
Pull me close when it is cold,
Shower me with love when my demons spit fire,
One day, I will be your nightingale,
In the disguise of a sparrow,
And I will commingle in you,
Having found the gem,
I will sing the song of the hidden treasure,
And fly carefree,
Sprinkling the priceless love from above.

88. Everything, but Love

I didn't know if commitment was a thing,
& Love was another,
For, I had learnt to accomplish the former task more than the later.
I was doing fine,
Sometimes, composing the chimes of my mind.
Reason to live to live to reason was the only thing that chased my life,
Until a love chariot landed me on a confusing planet.
They named it Love,
Where I had Roller coaster rides,
With some nice Human beings, as on Earth,
But,
I threw up nauseated,
Maybe, because, the air wasn't fresh,
Bounded to patriarchal seat belts,
Yet, I stayed, working on my forte,
But, I was fading,
Spinning along the wheels,
I threw up, again, the second time, the third & again,
Till I was out of the game,
Far from that world.
Today, I wish to do everything in life, but love,
& it's free to not find its ways.

89. Drafting Consolation

As seasons changed,

Days grew cold, waiting,

For just a tight, warm hug,

To fill the cracks of my heart,

And then,

All the silence around would feel right,

Along with innumerous unsaid things acknowledged.

My chaotic thoughts, like a jigsaw puzzle, would find ways for coherence,

With such pure a touch;

A bliss,

I wish to be showered upon.

90. You And I

I was a storm,
That gushed around aimlessly
& destroyed the good,
You came as a leaf,
And flew along with me,
I changed directions in fury,
You just followed my soul blindly,
Like a tune set for a rhythm,
I was the force,
And you took turns,
Sometimes, to either stand as a wall, to protect me,
Sometimes, you fused in me when I traveled like the wind,
As the time served itself on the plate.
I was the malicious speed,
That could have destroyed the greater me,
But you protected it, worshiped it,
As if you saw the deity of love inside,
Under the clouds of anger, aloofness, and its superiority.
I crushed things around,
And was about to crash myself,
With an emotional vacuum,
But you came as a savior,
You held me tight, embraced me with care & persevered my fury,
And saved me from my anomaly.

91. What Is Love?

Love is the peace refill,
When nothing fits the void in your heart,
It does,
It is the magnet that connects souls,
The freedom that lets you soar high,
In your unforeseeable present,
A bridge from one life to another,
The holy chemical,
That enlightens the true spirits that worship it unwittingly,
Sometimes, it is the strongest alloy,
That weighs relationships,
While at other times, it is the thinnest air,
That passes you by, before you breathe it.
If you still crave for it,
When solitude couldn't balm your anxious mind anymore,
Remember: "Love Is The Peace Refill".

92. If I Could...

If I could open the doors of my love's heart,

I would know the reason behind his feigned enmity with me,

I would know if his denial for my love was genuine,

Or he was protecting me from the monsters within him,

I would know if the beautiful feelings of love, innocence and togetherness, that I am blessed with, is universally angelic,

Or it is only half divine!

If my love was pure,

Or it was just an infatuation,

Just like with any other being.

If we are tied by the holy knot in heaven,

Or we just crossed each other's path,

To acknowledge the void,

When the other part of my heart slipped,

To travel along his'.

93. Gravity

I had grounded Alone for long enough,
Could you please borrow some of my gravity to pull me close?

94. Burnt

I have got scars on parts of me,
When I got burnt by sparks of love,
Several times, in life,
Now, I wish to live with love, again,
That doesn't leave marks, but puts me on fire,
And I keep burning,
Despite the changing seasons,
Till ashes free my soul.

95. Tinted Glass windows

I have been a beautiful piece,
Till he had seen me from being,
Inside a glass room,
With curtains of various shades per his mood,
That I had always resisted to fit in,
Because I am more than just a pretty thing,
But, only if he could break the glass,
He could see the real me,
He would know that I am not just an animated piece,
Or a thing from his imagination,
I am as real as a male masterpiece,
& I have equal respect for a sober chauvinist,
At a distance,
Whether he is alive or becomes extinct.

96. That Someone

Wish to be with someone,
Who doesn't hesitate to answer my ifs and buts,
With all logic, honesty, patience and love,
Embracing the insecurities behind such thoughts,

97. Monsters

If you let yourself explore the I in me,
I would show you my monsters,
There are days when I overlook the good,
And gulp poison,
I need you then, to hold me tight,
Before I spit the pain out,
And let me shatter in your arms,
And save me from the stage outside,
I would want you to be my armor,
And be my back if I fall.
And stroke my hair gently like the summer winds in the evening,
Till I have gray hair,
Till the last winter that freezes our affair.

98. Love Dome

I held his hands,
To build a shelter of love for us,
But I didn't notice that his hands were slippery,
And my care for him was an escape room,
I was joining the pieces of the moments lived,
To decorate the castle of love.
I stained myself with all the hues possible,
In the process of collecting joys for my home.
And bathed in its glory in this dome.

I was waiting for the light,
But he came to be rescued,
From the darkness that was consuming him from within,
I tried to ignite hope,
But it would have been successful,
Only if he had the belief in him,
Attuned to flight,
He escaped from his escaping cocoon too.
I waited, till I washed myself clean,
With a half built dome shrined,
Accepting why people say "love is blind".

99. How old is your love?

Some let love to old,
Then, they renounce from it,
Mine died in its youth,
When I was just building our castle,
& Dressing the sheets for our honeymoon
Since then, the hollowness within echo,
Of a vacuumed heart longing for warmth,
Of a blinding closeness attracted by trust,
Now, provoking me to rise,
To age with the ones,
Who let their love grow.

100. With the wind

I am ice, I am fire,
Nothing less,
Yearning on the verge of extremities,
To be taken along,
I sing; "sometimes, I am a wandering child,
Sometimes a nurturer,
It depends on the company.
No matter the time,
You will relish the stream,
The rocky climbs,
Or a steep road,
When we walk along."

101. When you come

Come to me like,
A breeze in the air,
Of such monsoons rare,
That mirrors rainbow in hearts,
Then embrace me in your whirls,
& carry me along to unlock the love fragrance.

102. Memories

In the gray times,
Memories send me some hues to the present,
I call them to relive with me,
They smile at me with empathy,
Cheering me up to be like them, one day,
I try to wear them like a dress,
To at least feel their feeling as they posted,
But they are happily framed in the time's game,
Each one of them positioned one after another,
Encouraging me to live the moment now,
& let the present click my poses,
To look poised in the near tomorrow,
When I go to my memory lane,
At times, when I fall short of colors.

103. Will You Be Mine?

I will rise everyday,
To conquer the world,
Spreading my wings far and wide,
And burn for your well-being,
Will you be my light?,
When I had lost mine,
Will you be my moon?,
& Stay by my side when it's dark,
And let me sleep with peace in your lap,
Some nights I can be a lone wolf,
And you rest under the soft clouds I bring,
That doesn't rain,
But cushion your anxiety to rest.

104. My Muse

Once, crowded thoughts knocked at the doors of my muse,
To be heard individually & diligently,
Once scattered, like the stars on a peaceful night,
Twinkling in their own light,
Now, have come along whispering in my ears,
Diligently, to wake me up from a deep slumber,
That is soothed by the balmy winds in the dark.
Disturbed by the commotion,
I question them, annoyingly, on the existence of the whole galaxy,
In my dreams,
They quieten up & stare at me gracefully,
As if they were mocking at my stupidity, silently,
For asking them something that I already knew answers of,
I waited for a response in my cracking sleep,
I also waited for it to break out of its cocoon, bit by bit,
To hear an answer from a starry galaxy,
Until I couldn't continue to feel the pleasing visuals,
And I woke up wide awake,
To find everything vanished.

105. Frozen

I am frozen with indifference to the reels of life,
And all I want is to flow in peace.

106. You

You are the reason for, having faith,
Living in moments,
Love passionately,
Embracing my monsters,
Believing in the universe,
Watering myself to bloom,
& to lead with poise.

107. One Liners

I

Some People leave us because; We cage them with the boundaries of our selfish needs.

II

Some people come to your life to become memories.

108. Truth Platter

Please bring some truth to the table,
Growing old has helped me like bitter gourd too,
There was a time when I loved sweets,
& I devoured them as soon as they came,
But then, I realized that it's not good for my heart!

109. Ode To My Best Of Pals

Spending time with you feels like,
The smell of shrunken berries,
That lay lethargic on a terrace,
Under the scorching sun of a summer noon,
Ready to be collected in a jar for pickles,
Ravens perch on the roof for a feast, cawing,
And fly away before anyone could see,
In the quietude of the countryside.
Laziness travel through the greenery,
To sing you a lullaby.
As the gentle winds push your daily agony for a while.

110. Don't Come too Close

Please don't come close,
It's freezing inside,
I want to melt away too,
But I don't want to douse your fire,
Of temporal desires in its fluttering flames,
With my cold winds,
I am an old stubborn ice of the age,
Leave it to sit as a hard rock piece,
To safeguard your heart from its chilliness.

111. Flattery

Flattery is cheap,
I have got a higher standard of living.
Of course, none expects a Debbie Downer either,
Truth is okay,
But you know better, how mediocres live!

112. She is Wild Waters

She is wild waters,
If you throw yourself into it,
Don't expect to be found,
Her calm waves may shelter your impulse,
For a while, you may fight against the force,
But you will relish to breathe the depth of an undisturbed home,
And lay there composed, serene
Safe from the chaos outside,
For she runs carefree,
Into people's hearts,
Her emotions gush within from her instinctive turbine,
To submerge the ones who come along.

113. A Goal

A Goal is not set during your mood swings,

But the time when you are ready for the marathon, after your warm ups.

114. Walkers Of Life

Dear walkers of life,
Stay eyed to your aim,
Hold on to your blistery feet steady for some more time,
Don't ripe yet,
Bring some friction,
To your life,
Don't slip away from your power,
Think of it a little more;
You got one life & a thousand million dreams,
Stored in the sky,
That visit you in your sleep,
& your one wish to accomplish them all,
Fades in the light,
Amidst the chaos of the day,
Dear walker,
If you step up today,
I believe, the winds would surely push you,
As the universe, at times, follows your vibe too,
It's the time & the space to climb up,
To come a little closer to the sky,
Relish a closer proximity of your dreams to your eyes,
After your long walks' sigh.
Today, do step up towards your sky.

115. Paralysed

I feel paralysed,
When my wings are clutched,
Happiness wane,
I dive aimlessly somewhere in the middle of the ocean,
Hoping to embrace the shore,
I can choose to drown,
But that's not what I am born for,
As that's when I become visible to the world,
Who would then declare me weak,
You know that it's the tradition of the universe,
To speculate and point at wrong doings first,
Blinded to all the white righteousness at the first glance.

116. Weight

I weighed a bagful of failures on one side,
And challenges of life on the other,
And I walked with a heart of feather,
To reach the place I wished to be,
My thoughts were born again, and again,
With my tanning actions,
As I soiled my hands, every day,
In the scorching reality of a corporate,
Till I grew a thick and dusky skin,
And armored my core with walls of wisdom,
I realized that fairness only exists in some fancy creams in packed boxes,
And some Television advertisements.
In reality, people either wear masks to prevent tanning,
Or they walked with pride with their dark skin.

117. I Wish To Be Found,

I Wish to be found
Amidst the time,
Where gravity only would mean to fall down while playing,
With cackles of laughter in the air,
Followed by band aids worn on hurt knees,
Cheery, sportive, artless,
Naive to the miseries of reality,
Or the worldly Pleasures.
Without being pulled in by the web of feigned treasures.

118. A Miser.

I was a miser,

Spending the charms of my cheerfulness diligently,

And saved the best ones,

For the one who would meet me unwittingly,

Till I met someone who seemed richer than me, handsome in his deeds,

I became a spendthrift after meeting him,

For I knew that we had enough for both of us to survive,

But I wasn't right,

One day, I was left bankrupt when I found him missing,

I pitied myself saying that it was still okay to live mediocre,

So, I looked into the treasure box to feed myself,

Only to find that it was empty.

My life was so damaged that I thought,
If I spoke my heart out, it would be trashed to nothing,
But as I whined,
My words weaved into poetry, to prove my thoughts wrong!

www.ingramcontent.com/pod-product-compliance
Ingram Content Group UK Ltd.
Pitfield, Milton Keynes, MK11 3LW, UK
UKHW042001230426
12048UKWH00009B/469